AF413206

Dreamers Like Me

Famous Hijabis Around the World

Written and Illustrated
by
Nora Mohtadi

Written and Illustrated by Nora Mohtadi
Edited by Sirah Jarocki

The illustrations featured in this book are graphically designed by
Nora Mohtadi, incorporating purchased works from various artists.

Includes bibliographical references | Audience 8 +. Subjects: Famous Muslim Women-
Biography-Juvenile Literature, Creative Nonfiction

Hardcover Edition - ISBN: 9798869352019
Hardcover Award Edition ISBN: 9798348513788

Printed in USA

This book is dedicated to all my sisters who have changed the world.

Ahlam nestled beside her father following the Maghreb prayer, staring at the moon as it began to rise. She tried to imagine what it was like in space and giggled.

"What are you thinking about?" asked Baba.
"What if I were an astronaut chef dancing on the moon?" Ahlam replied.

Baba laughed with her. After a minute, Ahlam grew quiet. "Do you think I could go to the moon? But what if I want to do something else? It's probably a lot harder than just daydreaming."

Her baba smiled. "Did you know that Ahlam means dreamer in Arabic? You are meant to dream of going to the moon or becoming a chef, or even both." Baba continued seriously, "Ahlam, it is our big dreams that help us decide what we want to be, but without hard work, they are just dreams."

Ahlam felt as though her dreams were still out of reach. "No matter how hard I try, it seems impossible," she sighed.

"It's not impossible," Baba insisted. "Many girls like you have achieved their dreams." He turned to his computer and started searching for pictures. "Let's research together. There are many inspirational dreamers who are just like you."

Burçin Mutlu-Pakdil

You can be a curious astrophysicist, like Burçin Mutlu-Pakdil, exploring new galaxies.

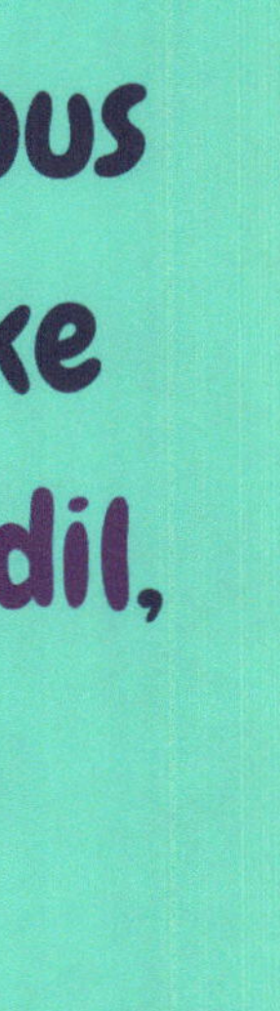

Discovering the unimaginable.

Turkish astrophysicist Burçin Mutlu-Pakdil discovered a new galaxy, which was named Burçin's Galaxy in her honor. She has received recognition from many respectable organizations and was named a "Woman of Impact" in National Geographic.

Sheikha Moza bint Nasser

You can be a
strong leader like
Her Highness Sheikha Moza,
creating opportunities for
all.

Spearheading
movements to
help empower
others.

Her Highness Sheikha Moza bint Nasser has been leading social and educational change in Qatar and around the world for many years. As one of the founders and leaders of the Qatar Foundation, Her Highness plays an important role in bringing forward new ideas and overseeing success in education.

Carolyn Walker-Diallo

You can be an honorable judge like **Carolyn Walker-Diallo**, upholding the law and delivering justice.

Becoming a voice for truth in the courtroom.

In 2015, Carolyn Walker-Diallo became the first hijabi American judge, taking her oath with the Quran. By 2019, she was recognized as one of Crain's Notable Women in Law, and in 2021, she became a judge for New York City.

Nadiya Hussain

You can be a masterful chef like **Nadiya Hussain**, baking sweets fit for a queen.

Mixing, baking, painting, and sculpting culinary art.

Nadiya Hussain, a British chef, won the sixth season of BBC's The Great British Bake Off in 2015 and baked Queen Elizabeth's 90th birthday cake. Today, she hosts a cooking show and has written cookbooks and children's books.

Ibtihaj Muhammad

You can be a fierce
athlete like
Ibtihaj Muhammad,
sharpening your craft,
and inspiring others.

Winning medals
and making
your country
proud.

Ibtihaj Muhammad made history as the first hijabi Olympic athlete to win a medal. A Barbie doll was modeled after her, and she has co-written children's books and appeared on TV talk shows.

Iqbal El Assaad

You can be a respected doctor like Iqbal El Assaad, having the power to help heal.

Making sure that your patients get the best care.

Dr. Iqbal El Assaad, a Palestinian refugee, finished high school at the age of 12 and received a scholarship from Her Highness Sheikha Moza. At 20, she graduated from medical school, becoming one of the youngest doctors and pediatric surgeons in the world.

Kübra Dağlı

You can be a master
of martial arts like
Kübra Dağlı,
demonstrating the
art of self-control.

Fighting with an
unbreakable spirit,
you can achieve
anything.

Kübra Dağlı is a Turkish Taekwondo athlete and two-time world champion. She has won the World Champion title twice and the European Champion title four times. Including her second and third place wins, she's earned seven European and seven World medals as of 2023.

Tawakkol Karman

You can be a brave activist like **Tawakkol Karman**, standing up for the rights of others.

Leading, fighting, and marching for a noble cause.

Tawakkol Karman, the "Mother of the Revolution," won the Nobel Peace Prize for standing up for women's rights in Yemen, becoming the first hijabi and Arab woman to receive the award. She continues to fight for women's freedom in Yemen today.

Nora Al-Matroshi

You can be a fearless astronaut, like Nora Al-Matrooshi defying gravity!

Traveling among the precious stars and planets.

Nora Al-Matrooshi, an Emirati engineer, made history as the first hijabi fully trained to go to space. In March 2024, she officially became a NASA Astronaut.

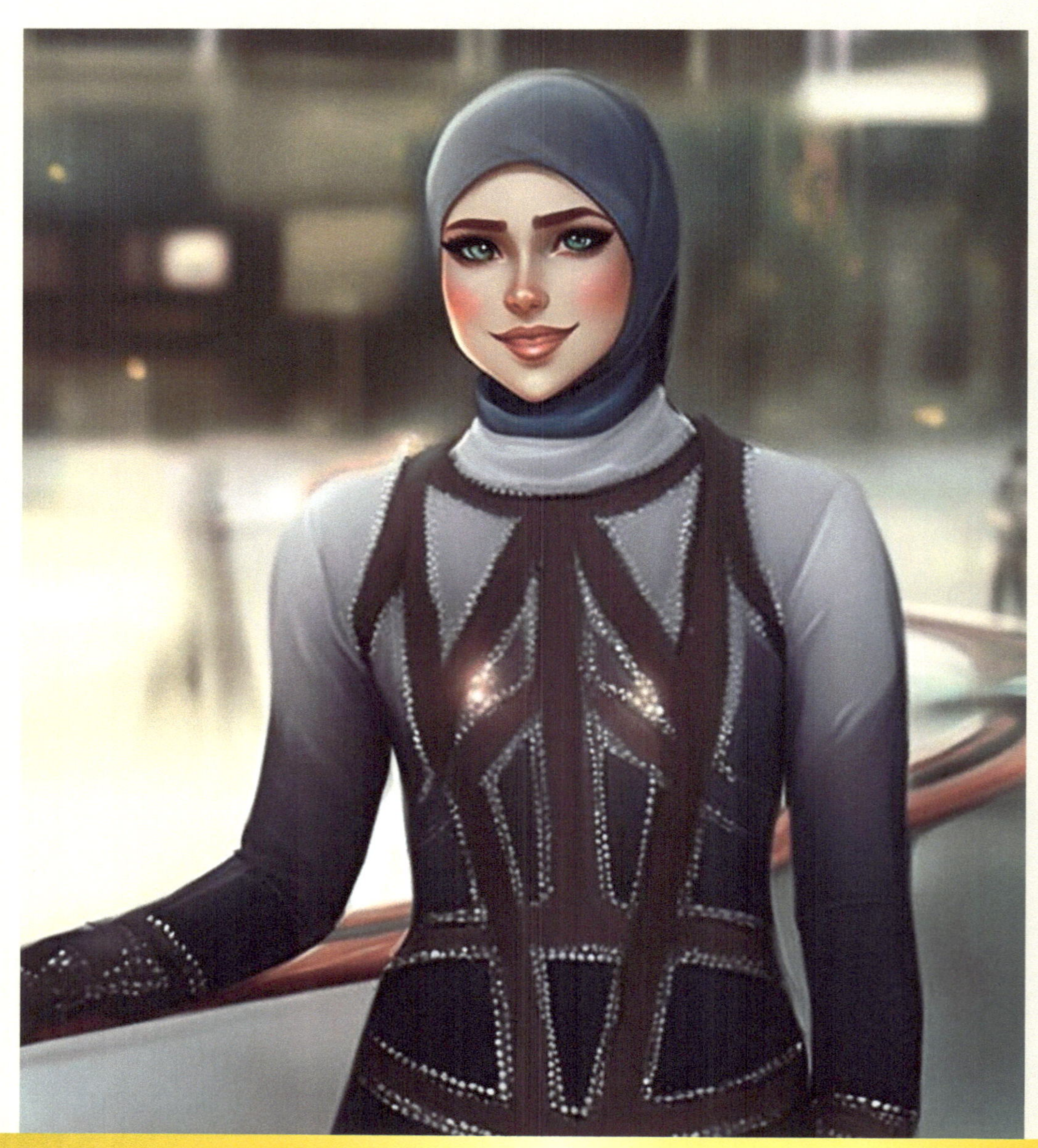

Zahra Lari

You can be a competitive
ice skater like
Zahra Lari,
following your dreams
with elegance.

Proving to the
world that you
can do
anything.

Zahra Lari is the first ice skater to win five championships while wearing a hijab and holds the world record for 63 spins on ice in a minute. She is currently the leader of the Emirates Skating Club and the president of the Figure Skating Committee in the UAE.

Tahera Rahman

You can be an ambitious reporter like **Tahera Rahman**, informing millions about global events.

Reporting on big issues with courage and a big voice.

Tahera Rahman is the first Muslim woman editor-in-chief and hijabi broadcast newscaster in the U.S. She has received the Illinois Broadcasters Association's Excellence Award. Currently, she reports for NBC 5 in Dallas-Fort Worth, Texas.

Maha Ayesh

You can be a mighty police officer like **Maha Ayesh**, keeping a community feel safer.

Maintaining peace and order.

Maha Ayesh is a detective with the Bartlett Police Department in Lombard, Illinois, and one of the few hijabi sworn officers in the U.S. She has a background in forensic psychology and is a licensed therapist.

Qorsho Hassan

You can be a dedicated teacher like Qorsho Hassan, educating children all year long.

Motivating young people to learn and grow.

Qorsho Hassan is a Somali-American educator who received a Fulbright scholarship to teach English in Malaysia. She was named the 2021 State Teacher of the Year in Minnesota and now leads Thrive Ed, focusing on student-centered education.

Shahnaz Laghari

You can be a daring pilot like **Shahnaz Laghari**, soaring through the air.

Proving to the world that nothing can stop you from reaching for the stars!

Captain Dr. Shahnaz Laghari is the first fully veiled, or niqabi, female pilot in the world, an achievement that earned her a spot in the Guinness World Records. She is known for empowering women in Pakistan through her community work.

Lena Khan

You can be an imaginative movie director like **Lena Khan**, bringing the magic of storytelling to life.

Captivating the audience with your imagination.

Lena Khan is a Canadian-American writer and director known for her film The Tiger Hunter, which was shown in over 70 cities and received praise from big news companies like The New York Times and Los Angeles Times. She earned an Emmy nomination in 2023 and recently directed Disney's Flora & Ulysses.

Hend Almatrouk

You can be a diligent architect like **Hend Almatrouk,** building strong structures.

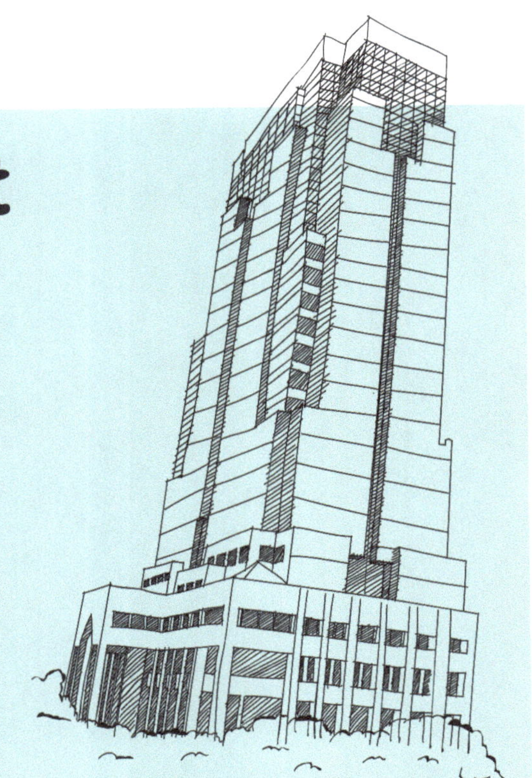

Managing teams of workers to bring your creations to life.

Hend Almatrouk is the leader of the award-winning architecture firm Studio Toggle in Kuwait and Portugal. In 2017, she was named Young Architect of the Year for her outstanding accomplishments and stunning building designs.

Halima Aden

You can be a confident fashion model like **Halima Aden,** showing the world how beautiful modesty can be.

Designing and unveiling gorgeous outfits for all to wear.

Halima Aden made history as the first hijabi semi-finalist in the Miss Minnesota USA pageant and the first to appear on the covers of many fashion magazines. She challenges beauty standards and stands for diversity in the modeling and fashion industry.

Huda Fahmy

You can be a creative writer like **Huda Fahmy**, publishing books that can be both funny and useful.

Letting your imagination run wild on every page.

Huda Fahmy is an Egyptian-American graphic novelist and teacher. Her 2023 National Book Award finalist, Huda F Cares?, uses humor and comics to explore the challenges many Muslim women in the West face.

Bilqis Abdul-Qaadir

You can be a passionate basketball player like **Bilqis Abdul-Qaadir**, playing with intensity alongside your team.

Strategizing and leading your team to victory.

Bilqis Abdul-Qaadir set the Massachusetts high school basketball scoring record with 3,070 points and played for the University of Memphis. She led a campaign for Muslim women's recognition in sports and met President Obama at the White House.

Aminah Shafiq

You can be an efficient engineer like **Aminah Shafiq,** finding unique solutions to problems.

Inventing new ways to advance the world.

Aminah Shafiq, an engineer with Severn Trent, created the first personal protective equipment (PPE) hijab in 2021, specifically for hijabi engineers. Her design earned her both the Water Industry Award and the British Muslim Award.

Stephanie Kurlow

You can be a graceful ballerina, like **Stephanie Kurlow**, floating across the stage to chase your dreams.

Performing fearlessly worldwide.

At age 12, Stephanie Kurlow became the world's first hijabi ballerina. She speaks out against online bullying, and in 2019, Stephanie partnered with Converse for a global campaign, reminding everyone that Muslim girls belong. Additionally, she appeared on the children's show The Wiggles in 2021.

WISe
Layla Shaikley

You can become an inventive software developer like **Layla Shaikley**, designing unique applications.

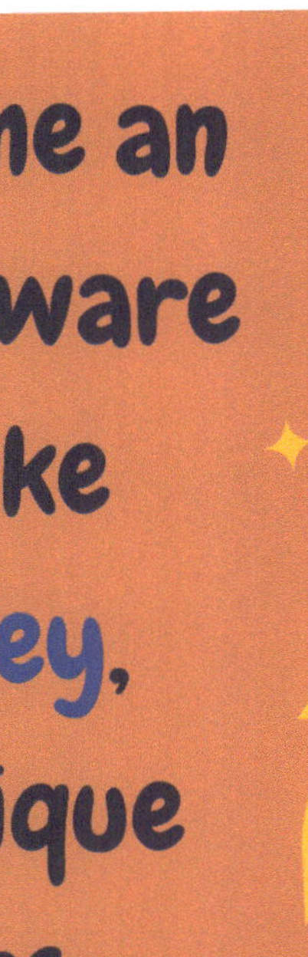

Developing global solutions through technology.

Layla Shaikley, an Iraqi-American, started her career at NASA in robotics and studied architecture at the Massachusetts Institute of Technology. Later, she started WISE Systems, a million-dollar software company.

Kameelah Janan Rasheed

You can be a vibrant artist like Kameelah Janan Rasheed, shaking up the art scene!

Showcasing your artwork in galleries and museums.

American artist and writer Kameelah Janan Rasheed won the 2021 Guggenheim Fellowship in Fine Arts and is recognized for her diverse art displays. She currently serves as the Arts Editor at SPOOK Magazine.

Sarah Al-Suhaimi

You can be an ambitious businesswoman like **Sarah Al-Suhaimi**, overseeing a financial empire.

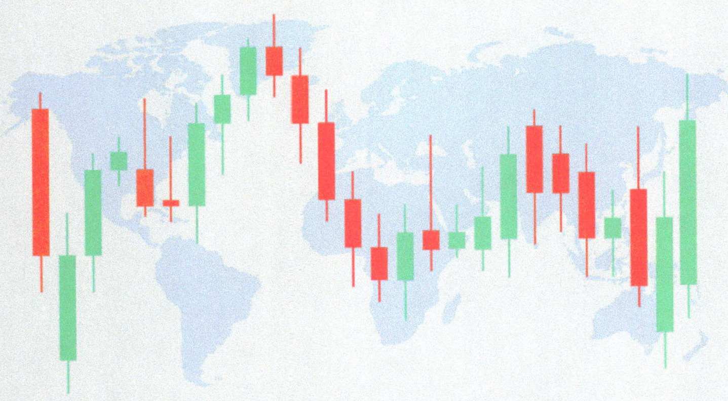

Making wise decisions for success worldwide.

Sarah Al-Suhaimi, a Harvard Business graduate, became the first chairwoman of the Saudi Stock Exchange in 2017 and significantly impacted Saudi Arabia's finance sector. In 2019, she was recognized as one of Forbes Magazine's top 100 women worldwide.

Halimah Yacob

You can be a resilient President like Halimah Yacob,

leading a country with compassion and courage.

Building lasting connections and impacting the world around you.

Halimah Yacob was Singapore's eighth president from 2017 to 2023, where she was known as "A President for Everyone." She focused on improving social systems in her country and created a positive image for Singapore globally.

Ahlam leaned away from the computer, her eyes sparkling as she thought about all the amazing Muslim women she had learned about. Baba proudly placed his hand on her shoulder. "So many amazing hijabi women started by just dreaming, then made their dreams come true. Ahlam, you can achieve anything you set your mind to. You are just like them."

Ahlam beamed. "I know it's going to take lots of hard work and tons of dreaming, but I think I could go to the moon and become a famous chef if that's what I want to do."

Baba grinned. "Who knows? Maybe one day another girl out there will need inspiration and will read about you chasing your dreams."

Sources

2021 State Teacher of the Year, Minnesota – Qorsho Hassan – Ntoy.ccsso.org. ntoy.ccsso.org/2021-state-teacher-of-the-year-minnesota-qorsho-   hassan/. Accessed 30 Apr. 2024.

"About Me." Nadiya Hussain, www.nadiyahussain.com/about-me/.

"Bilqis Abdul-Qaadir." The Black American Muslim, www.theblackamericanmuslim.com/bilqis. Accessed 30 Apr. 2024.

"Bio — Kameelah Janan Rasheed." Kameelahr.com, kameelahr.com/Bio. Accessed 30 Apr. 2024.

Brandman, Mariana. "Ibtihaj Muhammad." National Women's History Museum, 2022, www.womenshistory.org/education-resources/biographies/ibtihaj-muhammad.

"Burcin Mutlu Pakdil | Bio." Bmutlupakdil, www.burcinmutlupakdil.net/about-me.

"Carolyn Walker-Diallo, Muslim Judge, Sworn in on Koran in Brooklyn." New York Daily News, 17 Dec. 2015, www.nydailynews.com/2015/12/17/carolyn-walker-diallo-muslim-judge-sworn-in-on-koran-in-brooklyn/. Accessed 30 Apr. 2024.

"Halima Aden | One Young World." Www.oneyoungworld.com, www.oneyoungworld.com/counsellors/halima-aden.

"Halimah Yacob." The Muslim 500, themuslim500.com/profiles/halimah-yacob/.

Han, Yoonji. "I Fought for the Right to Wear the Hijab in Professional Basketball. I'm Finding Hope in Progress amid the Iranian Protests over Women's Right to Choose." Business Insider, www.businessinsider.com/bilqis-abdul-qaadir-hijab-muslim-basketball-iran-protest-mahsa-amini-2022-11.

Hend Almatrouk – Studio Toggle. studiotoggle.com/team/hend-almatrouk. Accessed 30 Apr. 2024.

"Hend Almatrouk – Tags | AmazingArchitecture." Amazingarchitecture.com, amazingarchitecture.com/tags/hend-almatrouk. Accessed 30 Apr. 2024.

"Her Highness Sheikha Moza Bint Nasser | Biography." Www.mozabintnasser.qa, www.mozabintnasser.qa/en/moza-bint-nasser/biography.

"History in the Making! Sarah Al-Suhaimi Becomes First Woman to Head Saudi Arabia Stock Exchange at 44." Www.india.com, www.india.com/women/history-in-the-making-sarah-al-suhaimi-becomes-first-woman-to-head-saudi-arabia-stock-exchange-at-44-6828039/. Accessed 30 Apr. 2024.

"Huda Fahmy." National Book Foundation, www.nationalbook.org/people/huda-fahmy/. Accessed 30 Apr. 2024.

Sources (Continued)

"Ibtihaj Muhammad." Biography, 14 Nov. 2017, www.biography.com/athlete/ibtihaj-muhammad.

"Iqbal El Assaad, MD." Cleveland Clinic, my.clevelandclinic.org/staff/29007-iqbal-el-assaad. Accessed 30 Apr. 2024.

"Iqbal El-Assaad Biography | Booking Info for Speaking Engagements." Www.allamericanspeakers.com, www.allamericanspeakers.com/celebritytalentbios/Iqbal+El-Assaad/442786. Accessed 30 Apr. 2024.

"Keeping the Peace While Keeping Her Faith, Muslim Officer Breaking Barriers." WGN-TV, 26 Apr. 2022, wgntv.com/news/cover-story/keeping-the-peace-while-keeping-her-faith-muslim-officer-breaking-barriers/. Accessed 30 Apr. 2024.

"Kübra Dağlı." Red Bull, www.redbull.com/us-en/athlete/kubra-dagli. Accessed 30 Apr. 2024.

"Layla Shaikley | Co-Founder + Product - Wise Systems." Forbes Technology Council, councils.forbes.com/profile/Layla-Shaikley-Co-Founder-%2B-Product-Wise-Systems/aaaed004-c532-4420-bdf3-9d38fc3c7e8d. Accessed 30 Apr. 2024.

"Lena Khan - Biography." IMDb, www.imdb.com/name/nm3414572/bio/?ref_=nm_ov_bio_sm. Accessed 30 Apr. 2024.

"Meet Aminah Shafiq, the Lady Busy Breaking Barriers for Muslim Girls around the World." The Phoenix Newspaper, 14 Dec. 2023, thephoenixnewspaper.com/meet-aminah-shafiq-the-lady-busy-breaking-barriers-for-muslim-girls-around-the-world. Accessed 30 Apr. 2024.

"Meet the First 'Arab Woman Astronaut' to Be Trained by NASA! All about Nora al Matrooshi." Www.businesstoday.in, 7 Mar. 2024, www.businesstoday.in/visualstories/news/meet-the-first-arab-woman-astronaut-to-be-trained-by-nasa-all-about-nora-almatrooshi-111833-07-03-2024. Accessed 30 Apr. 2024.

Mneimneh, Razan. "7 Facts about Stephanie Kurlow, the World's First Hijabi Ballerina." StepFeed, 27 Jan. 2020, stepfeed.com/7-facts-about-stephanie-kurlow-the-world-s-first-hijabi-ballerina-7707.

"Most Upright Spins While Ice Skating in One Minute." Guinness World Records, 30 Oct. 2023, www.guinnessworldrecords.com/world-records/754625-most-upright-spins-while-ice-skating-in-one-minute#:~:text=The%20most%20upright%20spins%20while. Accessed 30 Apr. 2024.

Secretariat, We-Fi. "Sarah al Suhaimi." Women Entrepreneurs Finance Initiative, 17 Sept. 2019, we-fi.org/sarah-al-suhaimi/. Accessed 30 Apr. 2024.

"Tahera Rahman." NBC 5 Dallas-Fort Worth, www.nbcdfw.com/author/tahera-rahman/. Accessed 30 Apr. 2024.

Sources (Continued)

"Tawakkol Karman Yemen." Nobel Women's Initiative, www.nobelwomensinitiative.org/tawakkolkarman.

"The Nobel Peace Prize 2011." NobelPrize.org, 2011, www.nobelprize.org/prizes/peace/2011/karman/facts/.

Times, Parkchester. Captain Shahnaz Laghari: Pioneering the Skies and Empowering Women – Parkchester Times. 23 Sept. 2023, www.parkchestertimes.com/2023/09/23/captain-shahnaz-laghari-pioneering-the-skies-and-empowering-women/. Accessed 30 Apr. 2024.

White, Gemma. "Emirati Figure Skating Champion Zahra Lari on What Being the First Means to Her." Vogue Arabia, 10 Apr. 2019, en.vogue.me/culture/zahra-lari-vogue-arabia-interview/. Accessed 30 Apr. 2024.

NORA MOHTADI

Nora Mohtadi, an educator and mother of four, noticed students' curiosity about her culture, prompting her to write. She authored "Hijabi ABCs" to promote the representation of modest girls and "Dreamers Like Me," which highlights 25 influential hijabi women and won the Regal Summit Award. Her latest book, "Super Yaseen!", was inspired by her twin autistic nephews, aiming to help children understand neurodiversity. With over 14 years of teaching, she seeks to inspire a love of learning and reading through her writing.

SIRAH JAROCKI

When adults would ask Sirah, "What do you want to be when you grow up?" Sirah would say, "I want to read books for a living." After a few chapters as a teacher and photographer, Sirah turned a page in life and is now quite comfortable helping authors bring dreams to life (and reading in every spare minute). Sirah loves many kinds of books and, of course, wouldn't be happy without a pile of picture books from the library every Friday afternoon. Sirah loves the way books can help create empathy, a little escape from the hard things, and moments of connection with diverse personalities.